LEARNING TO LOVE OURSELVES

learning to love ourselves

by Richard Peace

Second in a series
of Bible studies
on the fundamentals
of the Christian life

ZONDERVAN PUBLISHING HOUSE
GRAND RAPIDS, MICHIGAN

Grateful acknowledgment is made to the following publishers for permission to reprint copyright material:

ABINGDON-COKESBURY PRESS for excerpts from *The Interpreter's Bible,*
copyright © 1952 by Pierce & Smith.

GEOFFREY BLES LTD. (London) and THE MACMILLAN COMPANY (New
York) for excerpts from C. S. Lewis, *Mere Christianity;* and for
excerpts from J. B. Phillips, *The New Testament in Modern English,*
copyright © 1958 by J. B. Phillips.

WILLIAM COLLINS SONS & CO., LTD. (London) and FORTRESS PRESS
(Philadelphia) for excerpts from John Doberstein (ed.), *The Minister's Prayer Book.*

THE DIVISION OF CHRISTIAN EDUCATION OF THE NATIONAL COUNCIL
OF THE CHURCHES OF CHRIST for quotations from The Revised
Standard Version of the Bible, copyright © 1946 and 1952.

INTER-VARSITY FELLOWSHIP (London) and WILLIAM B. EERDMANS
(Grand Rapids) for the quotation from *The New Bible Dictionary.*

INTER-VARSITY FELLOWSHIP, TYNDALE PRESS (London) and INTER-
VARSITY PRESS (Chicago) for excerpts from James Denney, *The
Death of Christ.*

THE SAINT ANDREW PRESS (Edinburgh) and THE WESTMINSTER PRESS
(Philadelphia) for excerpts from William Barclay, *The Daily Study
Bible: The Letters to the Philippians, Colossians, and Thessalonians;
The Letter to the Romans.*

ZONDERVAN PUBLISHING HOUSE (Grand Rapids) for excerpts from
Eugenia Price, *Find Out for Yourself,* copyright © 1963.

FOREWORD

For several years I have watched with deep appreciation the growth of African Enterprise — a remarkable movement emerging from the vision of several outstanding young men. They are implementing with vigor, imagination, and spiritual power a burden to raise up an effective evangelistic tool in modern Africa. It has been my real privilege to serve on the Advisory Board of African Enterprise.

Now I am delighted to commend *Learning to Love* — a creative series of Bible studies by one of the African Enterprise team — Dick Peace.

Learning to Love is a first-rate piece of work. It will help to fill the growing need for effective evangelistic follow-up literature. This series is particularly fine in its balance. It is biblically and theologically mature. It presents basic Christian truth clearly, and at the same time is designed to force the student to think and learn for himself. Christian life and belief are woven together. The selected quotations and suggestions for further reading are excellent.

Obviously, Dick Peace and the African Enterprise team grasp the fact that evangelism is not an end in itself: decision for Christ is the doorway to discipleship. Commitment to Christ is not a one time affair: it is the start of a life of commitment. As Jesus said, "Come unto me . . . Take my yoke upon you . . . Learn of me." I pray that these studies may be used as follow-up for evangelistic missions, as a basis for Bible study groups in the home and among students, as an introduction to the Christian life for Sunday schools, and in many other ways to help people to love as Christ has loved us.

LEIGHTON FORD

Charlotte, North Carolina

TO JUDITH

PREFACE

The aim of any Bible study ought to be to bring the reader into contact with Scripture in such a way that his life will be changed. This is my aim in *Learning to Love*. The focus therefore is not on learning doctrine but on learning how to live like a Christian. Doctrine is there, of course, but always in relationship to life.

These studies were written originally to serve as follow-up literature for African Enterprise evangelistic missions. I am grateful for the opportunity these missions afforded to test out the material in live situations.

I am indebted to those who have helped me to produce these studies. My thanks goes to Michael Cassidy for his many suggestions and constant encouragement; to Dr. David Hubbard, President of Fuller Theological Seminary for suggesting these studies for publication; to Dr. Paul King Jewett, Professor of Systematic Theology at Fuller Seminary for his preceptive reading of the studies; and to Dr. Leighton Ford for kindly agreeing to write the foreword. I am grateful to Mrs. Kate Saunders for typing the original draft of the studies and to Miss Esther Kuun for her proofreading and typing of subsequent copies. My especial thanks goes to my wife Judy, not only for giving up so many of her evenings to the Bible studies but also for her encouragement and ideas.

Since the value of a book like this is greatly enhanced by reference to authorities writing on the general subject covered in each study, I acknowledge with thanks the publishers listed on the copyright page who have allowed me to quote from their books.

RICHARD PEACE

INTRODUCTION

The Christian life, some have said, is a life in which we *learn to love*. This series of Bible studies is designed to help you think about this life of love to which we have been called.

This series is based on an incident in the life of our Lord. One day a Jewish religious leader asked Jesus what the greatest commandment was (Mark 12:28-34). Jesus replied that the greatest commandment was to *love* God with all one's heart and to *love* one's neighbor as oneself.

We are going to examine love in these same three directions. The first five lessons will center around "Loving God." The second five will deal with "Loving Ourselves," while the concluding five will concern "Loving People."

HINTS ON USING THE LESSONS

These lessons will be of most value to you if you remember several things as you set out on this series.

First, work on these lessons in a quiet place where you will not be disturbed. These are intended to be Bible *study* lessons. You will not be able to study very well if people keep coming in and out of your room or if there is a nearby racket.

Second, don't be afraid to study. Study does mean a bit of work. But to be profitable these lessons ought not to be skimmed over. For the most benefit, you must spend time, read carefully, and think hard. The more effort you make, the greater the reward. And indeed the truths you discover from the Bible will be of inestimable value to you.

Third, keep these lessons private. If you know others will be reading your responses you probably won't be as honest as you can be in answering the questions. The more honest you can be, the more the Scripture can help you.

ANSWERING THE QUESTIONS

This is a series of *inductive* Bible studies. Inductive Bible study aims at leading an individual to discover *for himself* what the Scripture is saying. Hence the questions. They are intended to lead you to uncover for yourself the meaning of the passage.

This is an exciting method of study. You are not totally dependent on what others say about a passage. You can find out for yourself what it says. And once this method is grasped, it will enable you to study any passage of Scripture on your own.

Work at your own speed on the lessons. Spend as much time as you need to understand the significance of the passage.

FOR YOUR CONSIDERATION

There are two main spheres in which the Christian is meant to grow. The first is in understanding and the second in holiness. When he begins the Christian life, he probably understands very little and he has only just come to know God. Now he must increase in the knowledge of God and of his Lord and Saviour, Jesus Christ (Colossians 1:10; II Peter 3:18). This knowledge is partly intellectual and partly personal. In connection with the former, I would urge you not only to study the Bible but to read good Christian books. To neglect to grow in your understanding is to court disaster. The Christian way is strewn with such casualties.

We must grow also in holiness of life. The New Testament writers speak of the development of our faith in God, our love for our fellow men and our likeness to Christ. Every son of God longs to become more and more conformed in his character and behaviour to the Son of God Himself. The Christian life is a life of righteousness. We must seek to obey God's commandments and do God's will. The Holy Spirit has been given us for this purpose. He has made our bodies His temple. He dwells within us. And as we allow Him continuously to fill us with His power, He will subdue our evil desires and cause His fruit to appear, which is "love, joy, peace, patience, kindness, goodness, faithfulness, gentleness, self-control" (Galatians 5:16, 22, 23).

From *Basic Christianity*[1]
by John R. W. Stott;
London: Inter-Varsity
Fellowship; p. 139.
(Chicago: Inter-Varsity Press;
Grand Rapids: Wm. B. Eerdmans)

---

[1]In each lesson I have tried to choose a significant quotation which bears upon the theme of the lesson, and which will amplify and clarify the central concept.

CONTENTS

*Parts I and III are available from the publisher.

LEARNING TO LOVE OURSELVES

제목: 막 12:28-34

자아 사랑
"네 몸 사랑하듯"

LOVING OURSELVES

What do you think of yourself? Do you despise the day you were born? Do you wish you were someone else? Or, on the other hand, are you convinced that few people match up to you?

Both extremes are wrong, of course. Self-hatred is condemned by the Bible just as is pride. What we are called upon to do is to *love* ourselves. Proper self-love precludes both self-hatred and pride.

It surprises some people that the Bible advocates self-love. This is because such people equate self-love with pride. Yet nothing is further from the truth.

To see the difference let us analyze the primary passage which teaches this idea of self-love, Mark 12:28-34.

Then one of the scribes approached him. He had been listening to the discussion, and noticing how well Jesus had answered them, he put this question to him, "What are we to consider the greatest commandment of all?" "The first and most important one is this," Jesus replied —

"'Hear, O Israel: the Lord our God, the Lord is one; and thou shalt love the Lord thy God with all thy heart, and with all thy soul, and with all thy mind, and with all thy strength.'

11

The second is this,
'Thou shalt love thy neighbour as thyself.'
No other commandment is greater than these."
"I am well answered," replied the scribe. "You are absolutely right when you say that there is one God and no other God exists but him; and to love him with the whole of our hearts, the whole of our intelligence and the whole of our energy, and to love our neighbours as ourselves is infinitely more important than all these burnt offerings and sacrifices." Then Jesus, noting the thoughtfulness of his reply, said to him, "You are not far from the kingdom of God!" After this nobody felt like asking him any more questions. *J. B. Phillips*

A. Analysis

Fact[1]   1. Who approached Jesus?_____

Meaning   2. Try to discover from a Bible dictionary or elsewhere who the Scribes were and what they believed. (Incidentally, a good Bible dictionary is a prerequisite for any serious Bible study. Such a dictionary gives a host of information about words occurring in the Scripture.)

   _____

   _____

   _____

Fact   3. Who are the "them" to whom Jesus was speaking? Check the context (i.e. the sections before and after this passage) to find this answer.
Here is another important rule in Bible study: read the context before analyzing a passage. This will help to ensure a proper understanding of the portion under analysis.

   _____

---

[1]Remember that the "Fact" questions are those which can be answered *directly* from the passage, in the words of the passage. The "Meaning" questions are intended to draw out the implications of these facts and so cannot usually be answered by a direct quote.

Meaning   4. On the basis of your study of the word "Scribes," why do you suppose that this one was concerned about knowing the greatest commandment?

Meaning   5. Note that the first part of Jesus' reply, "Hear O Israel, the Lord our God, the Lord is one," is the central creed of Judaism. This is the sentence with which the synagogue service begins even today. In the midst of a society that worshiped a multitude of gods, the worship by the Jews of one God was striking.

Fact   6. How are we to love God?

    a) _____   b) _____

    c) _____   d) _____

Meaning   7. How can *you* love God with your whole heart and soul? What does this mean for you?

Meaning   8. How can *you* love God with your whole intelligence? What does this mean for you?

Meaning 9. How can *you* love God with your whole strength? What does this mean for you?

Fact 10. The second commandment tells us to love whom?

a)_____ b)_____

Meaning 11. From this second commandment, what gauge tells us if we are actually loving others as we ought?

Meaning 12. Who is your "neighbor"? Think about this carefully and prayerfully.

Meaning 13. To use the way we love ourselves as a standard by which to gauge our love of others implies that each of us has some notion of what proper self-love is. What is proper self-love then? Think and meditate carefully before answering.

Meaning 14. How do you feel about yourself? Do you know your strengths? Your weaknesses?

What are your strengths? _____

_____

_____

_____

What are your weaknesses? _____

_____

_____

_____

Does it make you proud that you have these strengths and others don't?

_____

Do you despair because of your weaknesses?

_____

_____

_____

Meaning 15. What do you suppose the difference between self-love and pride is?

_____

_____

_____

_____

_____

B. Significance

If we love ourselves properly we accept our strengths as gifts from God. We neither deny we are gifted (false humility) nor think ourselves superior because we may happen to be (pride). Nor do we imagine ourselves to be something we are not.

We also accept our weaknesses. We don't despair because of them. We try to overcome these weaknesses with God's help. We don't use them to get pity.

In other words, proper self-love begins with a *knowledge* and an *acceptance* of who we are.

Luke 9:23
let him deny himself ...

FOR YOUR CONSIDERATION

How much do you really respect yourself? Christians are often hammered at to "destroy self." This is not what Jesus said to do. He told us we were to love our neighbors as much as we love ourselves. How can we love a self we have destroyed? Actually, it is not even possible to do away with our *selves*. As long as we *are,* there will be our *selves*. True, we are to place our selves under the control of the Creator God (and who could know better how these selves should function?) but we are not to despise our *selves* or try to commit self-suicide. We are to be objective and clear-sighted about them and, after linking them to the very Self of God, go on to develop His creation to its maximum.

There is, of course, a right kind of self-love and a wrong kind. If you pamper yourself, you do not really love the essential you. Pampering always hampers. Jesus did not tell us to pamper either ourselves or our neighbors. He spoke of love; and love is creative and realistic and constructive. If we are cultivating our false selves, the self-seeking, self-preserving, distorted self which motivates all selfish behavior, we cannot expect anything but imbalance and bumps. God created man in His own image, and He created him into a human family. Families are supposed to get along together. When they don't, it is because false selves are being cultivated right and left. Each member of the human family has a definite particular contribution to make to the whole. I have mine, you have yours. When we learn to respect this fact in ourselves, we are then ready to begin to learn to respect it in the people we know.

From *Find Out for Yourself*
by Eugenia Price;
Grand Rapids: Zondervan
Publishing House; pp. 28 & 29.

FOR YOUR BOOKSHELF

1. *The Meaning of Persons* by Paul Tournier; New York: Harper
   & Row.
   A Swiss physician and psychiatrist with a deep Christian
   faith has written this exceptionally perceptive book which helps
   us understand ourselves and our motives. This book can
   change you.

2. *Escape From Loneliness* by Paul Tournier; Philadelphia:
   Westminster.
   A companion volume which centers on the inner loneliness
   which the author says all men experience. Both books help us
   to know ourselves. This is the first step to loving ourselves.

3. *Find Out for Yourself* by Eugenia Price; Grand Rapids:
   Zondervan Publishing House; especially pp. 23-32.
   Though written for young people, all will profit from the
   stimulation which this book gives one to think through the
   basic issues of life.

4. *What is God Like* by Eugenia Price; Grand Rapids: Zondervan Publishing House; especially pp. 155-168.
   This chapter (pp. 155-168) deals with accepting ourselves
   as we are.

KNOWING OURSELVES

Why is it that we seem to fail so often to keep our resolutions? On New Year's Day, perhaps, we resolve to study diligently all the next year. And we do study hard for the first few weeks. But then that feeling that we can't face the books any longer creeps in and we start putting off our study once more."

Or perhaps we resolve to be better parents and show more understanding to our children. Three days later we explode again over some silly thing which they have done.

Isn't it strange that we humans can often know the right thing to do — and still be unable to do it!

This brings us to the question of what man is like. Did you ever wonder what you were like inside? Why is it that you can want to do right but then fail so miserably?

The Bible has much to say about man's nature. Let us therefore look at a passage from the book of Romans which deals with this subject. By analyzing this section we ought to come to a better understanding of ourselves. When we understand our natures, then we can grasp what God has done for us and what He yet has to do. To love ourselves properly, as was pointed out in the last lesson, we must know ourselves. Here then is Romans 6:16-23:

You *belong* to the power which you choose to obey, whether you choose sin, whose reward is death, or God, obedience to Whom means the reward of righteousness. Thank God that you, who were at one time the servants of sin, honestly responded to the impact of Christ's teaching when you came under its influence. Then, released from the service of sin, you entered the service of righteousness. (I use an everyday illustration because human nature grasps truth more readily that way.) In the past you voluntarily gave your bodies to the service of vice and wickedness — for the purpose of becoming wicked. So, now, give yourselves to the service of righteousness — for the purpose of becoming really good. For when you were employed by sin you owed no duty to righteousness. Yet what sort of harvest did you reap from those things that today you blush to remember? In the long run those things mean one thing only — death.

But now that you are employed by God, you owe no duty to sin, and you reap the fruit of being made righteous, while at the end of the road there is life for evermore.

Sin *pays* its servants; the wage is death. But God *gives* to those who serve Him; His free gift is eternal life through Jesus Christ our Lord.

J. B. Phillips

A. Analysis

Fact   1. This passage pictures man as being in the service (or employ) of one of two contradictory powers. Underline each word in the passage which has to do with these ideas of service and employment. Remember service involves obedience, reward, wages, etc.

Here is another rule of Bible study: Underline similar words in a passage. This will help you to discover the theme of a passage.

Fact | 2. Now underline in a different color each "you" or "your" in the passage.

Surprising, isn't it, how often these words are used here. This means that the passage is for *your* benefit! *You* are the subject of the passage.

Fact | 3. What are the two powers to which we can give obedience?

a)_____ b)_____

Fact | 4. What are the rewards given to each type of obedience?

a)_____ b)_____

Fact | 5. What is the "reward of righteousness"? (Search the passage for this answer.)

_____

_____

Fact | 6. Each person belongs initially to what power?

_____

Meaning | 7. Now, according to question 6, what can you say about the *original* nature of man?

_____

_____

Meaning | 8. What do you suppose it means to "serve" sin?

_____

_____

_____

_____

Meaning 9. In what ways do you see that *you* (remember the subject of the passage!) now serve and have in the past served sin?

Fact 10. How is one released from the service of sin?

Meaning 11. When did you first begin to "respond to the impact of Christ's teaching"?

Fact 12. For what *purpose* does one give service to sin?

For what purpose service to righteousness?

Meaning 13. What sort of "harvest" did *you* reap from those things "that today you blush to remember"?

Fact 14. What is the ultimate harvest of sin?

Reread the passage slowly, bearing in mind all you have learned by answering these questions. Note how much clearer it is than it was on the first reading. In this way you will see for yourself why we must *study* the Bible if it is to become meaningful.

B. *Significance*

Now let us draw together the teaching in this passage about man's nature. Man starts out serving sin. This leads him into evil of all sorts and the final wage he receives for this service is eternal death (i.e. separation from God).

On the other hand, it is possible for a man to forsake the service of sin. Christ's death on the cross is the price sufficient to purchase a man from this master called Sin. Once purchased (and so we are when we commit ourselves to Christ), he enters the service of righteousness. The ultimate wage for such service is eternal life with God.

Many men never escape this service to sin and so they reap the results. Here on earth sin brings loneliness, broken relationships, unhappiness, wasted powers, etc. In the end it brings spiritual death.

But we can escape our sinful nature (and each of us starts out with a sinful nature) through Christ's power, which frees us to follow Right. In other passages of Scripture, we are told that when we become Christians we are given a "new nature" which inclines us to pursue right living.

Yet we are never totally free, while on earth, from this old, sinful nature. Becoming a Christian starts a war within us. Sin is reluctant to let us go, yet our new nature inclines us to do good and so the battle rages within us between good and evil. But we *do* overcome sin and are daily overcoming sin despite momentary giving-in to sin's persuasion.

We began this lesson by asking, "Why can we *want* to do right and then fail to do it?" The answer is that while our new nature inclines us to good, the old nature fights these impulses and often causes us to fail.

What is man's nature? At first it is inclined toward sin. But a new nature inclined toward good is given to those who ask it of Christ.

FOR YOUR CONSIDERATION

The Son of God became a man to enable men to become sons of God. We do not know — anyway, I do not know — how things would have worked if the human race had never rebelled against God and joined the enemy. Perhaps every man would have been "in Christ," would have shared the life of the Son of God, from the moment he was born. Perhaps the *Bios* or natural life would have been drawn up into the *Zoe*, the uncreated life, at once and as a matter of course. But that is guesswork. You and I are concerned with the way things work now.

And the present state of things is this. The two kinds of life are now not only different (they would always have been that) but actually opposed. The natural life in each of us is something self-centered, something that wants to be petted and admired, to take advantage of other lives, to exploit the whole universe. And especially it wants to be left to itself: to keep well away from anything better or stronger or higher than it, anything that might make it feel small. It is afraid of the light and air of the spiritual world, just as people who have been brought up to be dirty are afraid of a bath. And in a sense it is quite right. It knows that if the spiritual life gets hold of it, all its self-centeredness and self-will are going to be killed and it is ready to fight tooth and nail to avoid that.

Did you ever think, when you were a child, what fun it would be if your toys could come to life? Well suppose you could really have brought them to life. Imagine turning a tin soldier into a real little man. It would involve turning the tin into flesh. And suppose the tin soldier did not like it. He is not interested in flesh; all he sees is that the tin is being spoilt. He thinks you are killing him. He will do everything he can to prevent you. He will not be made into a man if he can help it.

* * * * * * *

The real Son of God is at your side. He is beginning to turn you into the same kind of thing as Himself. He is beginning so to speak, to "inject" His kind of life and thought, His Zoe into you; beginning to turn the tin soldier into a live man. The part of you that does not like it is the part that is still tin.

From *Mere Christianity*
by C. S. Lewis; Glasgow:
Fontana Book; pp. 150-151, 158;
New York: The Macmillan Co.;
pp. 139, 140; 148.
(Book IV, Chapters 5 & 7)

FOR YOUR BOOKSHELF

1. *Basic Christianity* by John R. W. Stott; especially pp. 61-82.
   Excellent summary of the fact and the consequence of sin.

2. *Mere Christianity* by C. S. Lewis; especially Book IV, Chapters 7-11.
   Very readable.

3. *Peace With God* by Billy Graham; especially pp. 37-52.

4. *Christian Doctrine* by J. S. Whale; especially pp. 33-50.
   A modern theological statement of the doctrine of sin.

5. *The Way of Holiness* by K. F. W. Prior; London: Inter-Varsity Fellowship; Chicago: Inter-Varsity Press.
   Chapter 4 explains the Biblical doctrine of sin as preparation for exploring the doctrine of holiness.

Lesson Eight

BEHAVING OURSELVES

"What marks out a real Christian is the way he lives." Ever hear someone conclude this? It is true of course that the experience of Christ changes a man's behavior.

But *how* ought our behavior to change? Some feel that we must become more austere. They feel our faces ought to lengthen and our smiles cease. They feel we should stop doing all sorts of things.

But this view leads to dull and rigid living. Rather Christianity ought to bring zest to life because our new patterns of living result in the first taste of real happiness we may ever have known.

Let's examine a portion of a letter which Paul wrote to the Church at Colossae. (Colossae was located in the Lycus Valley, notorious home of earthquakes, in what today is Turkey.) Paul writes in Colossians 3:1-17 of the life of the Old Nature and the life of the New Nature. Watch as you read for the contrasts between these two natures:

> If you are then "risen" with Christ, reach out for the highest gifts of Heaven, where your master reigns in power. Give your heart to the heavenly things, not to the passing things of earth. For, as far as this world is concerned, you are already dead, and

your true life is a hidden one in Christ. One day, Christ, the secret centre of our lives, will show Himself openly, and you will all share in that magnificent dénouement.

In so far then, as you have to live upon this earth, consider yourselves dead to worldly contacts: have nothing to do with sexual immorality, dirty-mindedness, uncontrolled passion, evil desire, and the lust for other people's goods, which last, remember, is as serious a sin as idolatry. It is because of these very things that the holy anger of God falls upon those who refuse to obey him. And never forget that you had your part in those dreadful things when you lived that old life.

But now, put all these things behind you. No more evil temper or furious rage; no more evil thoughts or words about others, no more evil thoughts or words about God, and no more filthy conversation. Don't tell one another lies any more, for you have finished with the old man and all he did and have begun life as the new man, who is out to learn what he ought to be, according to the plan of God. In this new man of God's design there is no distinction between Greek and Hebrew, Jew or Gentile, foreigner or savage, slave or free men. Christ is all that matters, for Christ lives in them all.

As, therefore, God's picked representatives of the new humanity, purified and beloved of God Himself, be merciful in action, kindly in heart, humble in mind. Accept life, and be most patient and tolerant with one another, always ready to forgive if you have a difference with anyone. Forgive as freely as the Lord has forgiven you. And, above everything else, be truly loving, for love is the golden chain of all the virtues. Let the peace of Christ rule in your hearts, remembering that as members of the same body you are called to live in harmony, and never forget to be thankful for what God has done for you.

Let Christ's teaching live in your hearts, making you rich in the true wisdom. Teach and help one another along the right road with your psalms and hymns and Christian songs, singing God's praises with joyful hearts. And whatever work you may have to do, do everything in the name of the Lord Jesus, thanking God the Father through Him.

J. B. Phillips

This lesson will probably best be tackled in two sittings. Do parts *A* and *B* the first day and part *C* on the second.

A. General Structure

Fact   1. In paragraph one, what are the two things to which one can give his heart?

a) _____

b) _____

Meaning 2. This *contrast* noted in question 1 forms the structure for the entire passage. Note that the first three paragraphs deal with the "things of earth," i.e. behavior by the "earthly-minded" man; while paragraphs 4 and 5 deal with the "things of heaven," i.e. behavior by the "heavenly-minded" man. The end of paragraph 3 contains the *transition* between these two contrasting ideas. To see this, underline in all five paragraphs the words "old" and "new."

In Bible study it is often best to read the whole passage first and try to discover the *structure*. Here the structure consists of presenting one idea, and then presenting the contrasting idea.

Note, too, the *transition* between these two contrasting ideas. Locating transitions is very helpful in tracing ideas.

Meaning 3. What phrase at the beginning of paragraph 3 serves as the transition between the idea of the old man and the new man?

_____

_____

_____

B. *Paragraphs 2 and 3*

Fact and
Meaning 4. List from paragraph 2 the words or phrases which describe those sinful things with which we, as Christians, are to have nothing to do. Then find the meaning of each word. A dictionary may help. By defining each word you will see more clearly what St. Paul means.

Word	Meaning
a) _____	_____
_____
b) _____	_____
_____
c) _____	_____
_____
d) _____	_____
_____
e) _____	_____
_____

Fact 5. What is God's attitude toward such things?

_____

_____

_____

6. Continue the above list by adding from paragraph 3 items not already mentioned in paragraph 2.

Word	Meaning
f)	....
	....
g)	....
	....
h)	....
	....
i)	....
	....
j)	....
	....
k)	....
	....

Meaning 7. Which of these words describe problems you have? If none of these fits your situation, what would you consider the area in your life most in need of transformation? Think and meditate. It is sometimes very difficult for us to face ourselves as we really are. *But remember, before we can change for the better, we must first see the areas which need changing.*

Meaning 8. Pray about your answer in question 7. Ask God to help you win the battle to change.

Fact and Meaning 9. Note the words "[you] have begun life as the new man who is out to learn *what he ought to be* according to the plan of God."

Have you ever wondered why some people who are openly anti-Christian seem to live far better lives than some Christians? This verse gives us insight into how this can be also.

Because of differences in background and circumstances, some individuals are by nature able to live better, more moral lives than others. Now suppose that a rather unlikeable individual from an unfortunate background becomes a Christian. His life, even though he is a Christian, will be lived at first on a lower level than a kindly pagan from a good home. This is because the new Christian has a lot "to learn about what he ought to be according to the plan of God." Becoming a Christian does not automatically make him perfect."

This sort of person may appear worse than the good pagan, but he is still in the process of *becoming* what he ought to be. Judge a man's Christianity not by where he is morally but by how much he has *changed*. (See *Mere Christianity,* Book IV, Chapters 10 & 11, for a fuller explanation of this idea.)

Fact 10. What does the new man think about people from different cultures and different races?

Fact   11. What binds men together as one? _____

_____

_____

_____

Meaning 12. How do you feel about people of other races and
            cultures? How has Christ affected your behavior
            in this area?

_____

_____

_____

_____

C. Paragraph 4

Fact and
Meaning 13. Thank God that you have been "picked" as a part
            of the "new humanity." How priceless a gift!

Fact and
Meaning 14. List the words or phrases in paragraph 4 which de-
            scribe what our behavior ought to be as representa-
            tives of the new humanity. Then find the meanings
            of each word. A dictionary may help.

Word	Meaning
a) _____	_____
	_____
b) _____	_____
	_____

c) _____   _____
                           _____

d) _____   _____
                           _____

e) _____   _____
                           _____

f) _____   _____
                           _____

g) _____   _____
                           _____

h) _____   _____
                           _____

i) _____   _____
                           _____

j) _____   _____
                           _____

k) _____   _____
                           _____

Fact   15. Note that most of these words deal with how we
           ought to live with other people. "There is no men-
           tion of virtues like efficiency, cleverness, even dili-
           gence and industry — not that these things are not
           important, but the great basic Christian virtues are
           the virtues which govern and set the tone of hu-
           man relationships."[1]

---

[1]*The Letters to the Philippians, Colossians, and Thessalonians* (*The Daily Study Bible*), Edinburgh: The Saint Andrew Press; Philadelphia: The Westminster Press; 1959; p. 188. See this section for a superb study of each word as to its meaning in the Greek original.

Meaning 16. How can *you* become more "merciful," "kind" and "humble"?

Fact and
Meaning 17. We often get angry and upset with others, particularly with those we may think to be our inferiors (e.g. children, employees, etc.). How ought we to behave with such?

How do you shape up here?_____

Fact and
Meaning 18. If you disagree with someone (and all of us do at one time or another) what should be the end result of this disagreement?

Why can we forgive others?_____

Are you ready to forgive:

    your husband or wife?_____

    your child? _____

34

your parents? --

your servant? --

your employer? --

your employee? ---

If not, ask yourself why not and pray over this until you can. Don't let anything, least of all pride, spoil any relationship.

If someone comes to you and asks *your* forgiveness for something, how do you react? Do you remain rather superior and act as if it's about time they said they were sorry? (Remember — very rarely is only *one* person at fault.) Or do you accept their request for forgiveness and, in turn, ask them to forgive you for your part in the misunderstanding?

Is there any relationship that needs to be healed? There can be no better day than today to start setting things right.

Fact   19. What one word sums up best what our whole behavior ought to be?

----

20. Now look back over the lessons. What is the main thing you have learned? Single out what has been personally significant to you. Jot it down here and begin praying about it.

FOR YOUR CONSIDERATION

When a man becomes a Christian there ought to be a complete change in his personality. He puts off his old self, and puts on a new self just as the candidate for baptism puts off his old clothes and puts on a new white robe. We very often evade the truth on which the New Testament insists, the truth that a Christianity which does not change a man is a most imperfect Christianity. Further, this change is a progressive change. This new creation is a continual renewal. It makes a man grow continually in grace and knowledge until he reaches that which he was meant to be — manhood in the image of God. Christianity is not really Christianity unless it recreates a man into what he was meant to be.

One of the great effects of that Christianity is that it destroys the barriers which divide. In it there is neither Greek nor Jew, circumcised nor uncircumcised, barbarian, Scythian, slave nor free man. . . .

It destroyed the barriers which come from birth and from nationality. Different nations, who either despised or hated each other, were all drawn into the one family of the Christian Church. . . .

It destroyed the barriers between the cultured and the uncultured . . . The greatest scholar in the world and the simplest son of toil in the world can sit in perfect fellowship in the Church of Christ.

It destroyed the barrier between class and class. The slave and the free man came together in the Church. . . .

To the garments of the virtues and the graces Paul adds one more — what he calls *the perfect bond of love*. Love is the binding power which holds the whole Christian body together. The tendency of any body of people is sooner or later to fly apart; and love is the one bond which will hold them together in unbreakable fellowship.

Then Paul uses a vivid picture. "Let the peace of God," he says, "be the decider of all things within your heart." Literally what Paul says is "Let the peace of God be the umpire in your heart." The verb he uses is a verb from the athletic arena; it is a word that is used of the umpire who settled things with his decision in any matter of dispute. If the peace of Jesus Christ is the umpire in any man's heart, then, when feelings clash, and when we are pulled in two directions at the same time, when Christian charity conflicts in our hearts with unchristian irritation and annoyance, the decision of Christ will keep us in the way of love, and the Church will remain the one body it was meant to be. The way to right action is to appoint Jesus Christ as the arbiter between the conflicting emotions in our hearts; and if we accept His decisions, we cannot go wrong.

> From *The Letters to the Philippians,*
> *Colossians, and Thessalonians;*
> translated and interpreted by
> William Barclay;
> Edinburgh: The Saint Andrew
> Press; Philadelphia: The Westminster
> Press; 1959; pp. 185-187; 190-191.
> Used by permission.

FOR YOUR BOOKSHELF

1. *Consistent Christianity* by Michael C. Griffiths; London: Inter-Varsity Fellowship; Chicago: Inter-Varsity Press.

   An excellent introductory study of the subject of Christian behavior. The book discusses such things; the family, sex, words, thought, etc.

2. *Making Men Whole* by J. B. Phillips; London: Fontana Books; New York: The Macmillan Co.; especially Part IV, "Inner Resources for the Task."

   The section noted is a discussion of the inner resources we have for living the Christian life, written by the man who did the excellent translation of the New Testament.

3. *Mere Christianity* by C. S. Lewis; Book III and Book IV, Chapters 10 and 11.

   Lewis's understanding of Christian behavior makes exciting sense.

4. *Your Confirmation*; pp. 79-116.

5. *Find Out for Yourself*; by Eugenia Price; pp. 143-154.

Lesson Nine

FORGIVENESS FOR OURSELVES

We have discovered in our lessons that as men we have two natures; an old nature which inclines us toward sin and a new nature which inclines us toward goodness. These two natures war within us. And even though we are winning the fight against sin, the war has its temporary reverses and we do commit sins as Christians.

What happens when we sin? Does God get angry and dislike us? Does He demand that we do difficult things to appease Him? Or does He just close His eyes to our sin and act as if nothing has happened?

These are vital questions. Let's look at what John says about sin in I John 1:5-9:

> 5 This then is the message which we have heard of him, and declare unto you, that God is light, and in him is no darkness at all.
>
> 6 If we say that we have fellowship with him, and walk in darkness, we lie, and do not the truth:

⁷ But if we walk in the light, as he is in the light, we have fellowship one with another, and the blood of Jesus Christ his Son cleanseth us from all sin.

⁸ If we say that we have no sin, we deceive ourselves, and the truth is not in us.

⁹ If we confess our sins, he is faithful and just to forgive us our sins, and to cleanse us from all unrighteousness.

Authorized (*King James*) *Version*

A. *Structure*

In our last lesson we began speaking about the *structure* of a passage. To see how an author has structured his writing is often a great help in understanding *what* he is trying to say to us.

In this passage, let's delve deeper than usual into the structure. The way we go about this is the very same way one would analyze the structure of any passage.

1. Read the whole passage and circle the word John uses to begin all but the fifth verse.

2. In verse 5 the opposite sides of a truth are given us. On the positive side we are told that God *is* light. On the negative side, we learn God *is not* darkness. "Light" is the one side, "darkness" is the other.

   Note too that in verse 6 the negative side of a truth is given and that in verse 7 the positive side of the same truth is presented. Both verses are introduced by the same word.

   Note that this is also true of the relationship between verses 8 and 9.

3. Let's chart the negative side of this main truth. Compare the two negative verses:

39

Initial 3 words	What?
Example:	
vs. 6 *If we say . . .*	*we have fellowship with Him while we walk in darkness . . .*
vs. 8 ------------------------	--------------------------------------

Then What?	"And" What?
vs. 6 *We lie . . .* and	*do not live according to the truth*
vs. 8 ------------------ and	------------------------------------

Look over this chart and note carefully the parallels you see.

4. Now do the same for the positive side of the truth:

Initial 2 words	"Do" What?
vs. 7 ------------------------	--------------------------------------
vs. 9 ------------------------	--------------------------------------

Then What?	"And" What?
vs. 7 ------------------------ and	--------------------------------------
vs. 9 ------------------------ and	--------------------------------------

40

5. The phrase, "if we say," which introduces both verse 6 and verse 8 is used to indicate a false teaching. We know that these are false teachings because they are followed by the phrases "we lie" (vs. 6) or "we deceive ourselves" (vs. 8).

Note these teachings. The first error (vs. 6) is to say that our behavior has nothing to do with our fellowship with God. The correcting statement in vs. 7 indicates that a pure life is necessary for fellowship with God.

The second error (vs. 8) is to say that men do not have a sinful nature. The correcting statement in verse 9 indicates that we have a sinful nature but we can be forgiven.

B. *Meaning*

We have looked more intensively than usual at the structure of this passage. Now, what does this passage *mean?*

Meaning   6. What does John mean when he says that God is *light?* What is light like?

Meaning   7. What then is the "darkness"? ------------------------

----

Fact   8. Why can we have no fellowship with God when we walk in darkness?

Fact 9. When we "walk in the light" we have fellowship not only with God but with whom else?

Fact 10. Through what do we receive forgiveness for our sin?

Meaning 11. Note that in verse 7 the singular "sin" is used while in verse 9 the plural "sins" is spoken of. What is the difference between our "sin" and our "sins"? (Hint: one has to do with our nature, the other with the conduct which results from our nature.)

Fact and
Meaning 12. Verse 9 is a key verse in the New Testament. We began our lesson by asking what happens when we sin. This verse answers our question.

a) Note that this verse *assumes* we will sin.

b) If we sin, what must we do? -----------------

----

c) To confess our sins means "to acknowledge sin and guilt in the light of God's revelation and this is generally an outward sign of repentance and faith."[1] This confession does not mean saying we are sorry in a mechanical way when we really aren't concerned over our sin. It involves repentance which is a sorrow over and a turning away from sin.

---

[1] *New Bible Dictionary;* London: Inter-Varsity Fellowship; Grand Rapids: Wm. B. Eerdmans; p. 247.

d) What will God do when we confess our sins?

1) _____

2) _____

e) What part of His nature causes Him to do this?

_____

f) Have you realized the marvel of this promise?
God actually offers to forgive you when you fail.
Not only that, He also promises to cleanse you
from this sin. Do you avail yourself each day of
this promised forgiveness?

_____

g) Memorize verse 9.

C. Temptation

But how do we slip into sin? At times (though by no means
always) we are confronted with an obvious choice between doing the right thing or doing the wrong thing. We have two possible ways to act. We deliberately choose either one or the other.
In such cases we are well aware of the right way but we are
tempted to follow the evil way. For example, you may know
that a certain book will have a bad influence on you. It is certain
to bring unhealthy and unclean thoughts. Your choice is to read
it. You are *tempted* to read it. Are you powerless in such situations? Must you yield to the temptation?

Here is I Corinthians 10:12-13:

[12] Therefore let anyone who thinks that he stands take heed lest
he fall.
[13] No temptation has overtaken you that is not common to man.
God is faithful, and He will not let you be tempted beyond your
strength, but with the temptation will also provide the way of
escape, that you may be able to endure it.

Revised Standard Version

Meaning 13. Ever feel that you are above some sin or another? Read verse 12. In *every* man is the capacity to commit *every* form of evil. Humbly recognizing this often spares one the agony of discovering too late that one was capable of doing it.

A young unmarried woman was weeping in the office of her doctor, a woman, who had just told her that she was pregnant. "But I can't be," she cried, "I'm not that kind of girl." The doctor's reply was "Young lady, we are *all* that kind of girl."

Thinking that we can stand is the sin of what?

Humbly recognizing our sinful inclinations is the first and essential step to overcoming sin.

Fact 14. Are your temptations unique?

Remember, *every* temptation which bothers you has bothered others. We hide our temptations from one another so we often don't realize this.

Fact 15. How will God help us to face and overcome temptation?

a) ---

b) ---

Remember, in *every* temptation you can escape if you really want to do so.

Fact   16. One "way of escape" is the sharing of your temp-
             tation with another. More than likely, this other
             person has faced the same thing (see question 12).
             What other "ways of escape" are there?

D. Conclusions

Temptation is sometimes obvious. But more often than not
our sinning is not a result of a clear-cut choice. It is a result of
reaction.

For example, someone does a stupid thing and we lash back
at them in anger. Ever do this to your children? No premedita-
tion here, just the natural response of our old nature.

What do we do? Recognize our sin, confess it, and accept
God's forgiveness. (Remember I John 1:9.)

This is why we need time each day to stop and recall
our activities. As we meditate we begin to see what we have
been like that day. We realize that at times our words were
spoken out of wrong motives. We may find we haven't been
quite honest in some discussion. Or we see that our behavior
toward a particular person was less than loving. When we
realize our sins we can ask for forgiveness and receive it.

Then when we have asked for forgiveness we must accept it.
Some people live with tremendous guilt feelings for years on
end. Yet God has said He will forgive *all* our sins. None are
excepted. If you ask for forgiveness, *trust* that you have received it.

Here is a prayer which you might find helpful as you think
over your day.

Forgive my sins, O Lord — forgive me the sins of my present and
the sins of my past, the sins of my soul and the sins of my body;
the sins which I have done to please myself, and the sins which

45

I have done to please others. Forgive me my wanton and idle sins, forgive me my serious and deliberate sins, forgive me those sins which I know and those sins which I know not, the sins which I have laboured so to hide from others that I have hid them from my own memory. Forgive them, O Lord, forgive them all. Of Thy great mercy let me be absolved, and of Thy bountiful goodness let me be delivered from the bonds of all that by my frailty I have committed. Grant this, O Heavenly Father, for the sake of Jesus Christ, our blessed Lord and Saviour. Amen.[1]

---

[1]*The Minister's Prayer Book*; John Doberstein (ed.); London: Collins p. 37. (Philadelphia: Fortress Press.)

FOR YOUR CONSIDERATION

Christ died for sins once for all, and the man who believes in Christ and in His death has his relation to God once for all determined not by sin but by the atonement. The sin for which a Christian has daily to seek forgiveness is not sin which annuls his acceptance with God and casts him back into the position of one who has never had the assurance of the pardoning mercy of God in Christ. On the contrary, that assurance ought to be the permanent element in his life. The forgiveness of sins has to be received again and again as sin emerges into act. But when the soul closes with Christ the propitiation, the assurance of God's love is laid at the foundation of its being once for all. It is not to isolated acts it refers, but to the personality; not to sins, but to the sinner; not to the past only, in which wrong has been done, but to time and eternity.

There will inevitably be in the Christian life experiences of sinning and of being forgiven, of falling and of being restored. But the grace which forgives and restores is not some new thing, nor is it conditioned in some new way. It is not dependent upon penitence, or works, or merit of ours. It is the same absolutely free grace which meets us at the cross. From first to last, it is the blood of Jesus, God's Son, which cleanses from sin. The daily pardon, the daily cleansing, are but the daily virtue of that one all-embracing act of mercy in which, while we were yet sinners, we were reconciled to God by the death of His Son.

From *The Death of Christ*
by James Denney;
London: Tyndale Press;
Chicago: Inter-Varsity Press;
p. 162.

FOR YOUR BOOKSHELF

1. *The Christian's Experience of Forgiveness* by H. R. Mackintosh; London: Fontana.
A thorough (and often deep) study of the doctrine of forgiveness.

2. *The Death of Christ* by James Denney; London: Tyndale Press; Chicago: Inter-Varsity Press.
A classic statement of the doctrine of atonement. This book requires vigorous study but more than repays the effort to master it.

3. *What Is God Like* by Eugenia Price; pp. 33-90.

4. *Find Out for Yourself* by Eugenia Price; pp. 155-164.

5. *Henceforth* by H. E. Hopkins; pp. 27-34.
Temptation is discussed.

6. *The Way;* by Robinson and Winward; pp. 42-49.
Again temptation is the topic.

7. *The Way of Holiness* by K. F. W. Prior; London: Inter-Varsity Fellowship; Chicago: Inter-Varsity Press.
Clarifies differences between justification and sanctification. Especially chapters 5, 6, and 7.

Lesson Ten

FREEDOM FOR OURSELVES

Some things are definitely right, others are definitely wrong. It's right to love your wife; it's wrong to beat her. It's right to speak the truth; it's wrong to lie.

But most of our choices in life are not so clear-cut. The decisions we are called upon to make are not all black and white. In fact, most of the choices we are faced with each day fall into that gray area of uncertainty, where it is difficult to know just what *is* right

For example, is it right to eat a second helping of mashed potatoes? The Bible says nothing about second helpings. What is the right thing to do? For the thin person a second helping may be a necessity. For the fat fellow, on the other hand, a second helping may just aggravate his weight problem and it could be sin for him to accept more mashed potatoes. Perhaps weight is not the issue. If you take the second helping, someone who did not have a first helping will be left mashed-potato-less!

Complex isn't it? But most of our daily decisions are no more clear-cut. Are there, therefore, any *guidelines* to help us in choosing correctly?

There are guidelines indeed. In Romans 14, which we will

consider in this lesson, you will find a most comprehensive discussion of how to choose properly in these gray areas. This is a longer passage than usual so we will not delve as deeply as is possible when only a few verses are analyzed. Incidentally, both types of Bible study are vital, i.e. study in depth of a few verses (as in lesson nine) or study of the main points of a long passage (as in this lesson).

The background to this chapter will help you in understanding it. The problem which stimulated Paul to write Romans 14 was whether or not a Christian could eat meat that had been offered to idols. In a city as great as Rome "much of the meat offered for sale had probably been sacrificed to idols. Could a Christian eat it with a clear conscience, or had evil associations contaminated the food?"[1] In answering this question Paul helps us to understand the concept of Christian freedom.

As you read the passage now, make a list below of those principles which will help you choose the right path when the decision is not obvious. (Don't worry if you find only one or two principles now and not seven.)

Romans 14

1 As for the man who is weak in faith, welcome him; but not for disputes over opinions. 2One believes he may eat anything, while the weak man eats only vegetables. 3Let not him who eats despise him who abstains, and let not him who abstains pass judgment on him who eats, for God has welcomed him. 4 Who are you to pass judgment on the servant of another? It is before his own master that he stands or falls. And he will be upheld, for the Master is able to make him stand.

5 One man esteems one day as better than another, while another man esteems all days alike. Let every one be fully convinced in his own mind. 6 He who observes the day, observes it in honour of the Lord. He also who eats, eats in honour of the Lord, since he gives thanks to God, while he who abstains, abstains in honour of the Lord and gives thanks to God. 7 None of

[1]Gerald R. Cragg, *The Interpreter's Bible, Vol. IX;* Nashville: Abingdon Press; p. 613.

us lives to himself, and none of us dies to himself. [8] If we live, we live to the Lord, and if we die, we die to the Lord; so then, whether we live or whether we die, we are the Lord's. [9] For to this end Christ died and lived again, that he might be Lord both of the dead and of the living.

[10] Why do you pass judgment on your brother? Or you, why do you despise your brother? For we shall all stand before the judgment seat of God;
[11] for it is written,

> "As I live, says the Lord,
> every knee shall bow to me,
> and every tongue shall give praise
> to God."

[12] So each of us shall give account of himself to God.
[13] Then let us no more pass judgment on one another, but rather decide never to put a stumbling block or hindrance in the way of a brother. [14] I know and am persuaded in the Lord Jesus that nothing is unclean in itself; but it is unclean for any one who thinks it unclean. [15] If your brother is being injured by what you eat, you are no longer walking in love. Do not let what you eat cause the ruin of one for whom Christ died. [16] So do not let what is good to you be spoken of as evil. [17] For the kingdom of God does not mean food and drink but righteousness and peace and joy in the Holy Spirit; [18] he who thus serves Christ is acceptable to God and approved by men. [19] Let us then pursue what makes for peace and for mutual up-building. [20] Do not, for the sake of food, destroy the work of God. Everything is indeed clean, but it is wrong for any one to make others fall by what he eats; [21] it is right not to eat meat or drink wine or do anything that makes your brother stumble. [22] The faith that you have, keep between yourself and God; happy is he who has no reason to judge himself for what he approves. [23] But he who has doubts is condemned, if he eats, because he does not act from faith; for whatever does not proceed from faith is sin.

Revised Standard Version

A. Analysis

Principles to Guide Our Choices

1) _____
2) _____
3) _____
4) _____
5) _____
6) _____
7) _____

Verses 1-4

Fact   1. What two opposite types of men are mentioned (or implied) in this first paragraph?

       a) _____

       b) _____

Fact   2. What behavior characterizes each?

       type a)_____

       type b)_____

Fact   3. How should the one act toward the other and vice versa?

       _____

       _____

       Why? _____

       _____

52

Meaning   4. How do you react to a person who holds the exact opposite opinion to you and firmly believes he is right and you are wrong?

Meaning   5. List those with whom you have such differences. Pray about your attitude toward them.

Verses 5-9

Fact   6. What new problem is introduced in verse 5?

Fact   7. What motivates both men to observe certain days the way in which they do?

Fact   8. Two men may decide differently about the observance of days. Which man is right?

What principle must guide *us* as to how we decide such issues for ourselves? (verse 5)

Meaning   9. This is the *first great principle* which ought to guide our conduct. "Each man must be fully satisfied in his own mind that his approach to the problem is right, i.e. the claims of conscience are sovereign."[2]

Take the mashed potatoes again. You must be convinced that your decision is right. If you eat the second helping you ought not to have any real doubts about the wisdom of doing so.

Verses 10-12

Fact   10. What are we *not* to do to those with whom we disagree?

a) ------

b) ------

Meaning 11. Do either of these attitudes describe your feelings about those with whom you disagree? If so, pray about your attitude and begin to set it right.

------

[2]*Ibid.*

Fact   12. Verse 14 presents the basis for the Christian's view
            that he is free from rules and regulations. What is
            it that gives him this conviction?

Meaning 13. What does Paul mean when he says that "nothing
            is unclean in itself"?

Fact and
Meaning 14. Though "fully convinced" in ourselves which is the
            right path to follow, sometimes our actions need
            even further tempering. Verse 15 gives us the
            second great principle for guiding our conduct.
            What is this principle? Write this out in your own
            words rather than just quoting verse 15.

            Back to mashed potatoes! I may feel it is quite
            proper to take a second helping, but I still might
            not do so if, by taking it, I harm another. Perhaps
            there is someone at the meal who is finding it diffi-
            cult to stick to a diet. My indulgence might cause
            them to toss over their diet and dig in — to their
            harm.

William Barclay gives another example of how this principle works.

> One man will genuinely see no harm in playing some outdoor game on the Sunday; and he may be right; but another man's whole conscience is shocked at such a thing, and, if he were persuaded to take part in it, all the time he would have the lurking and haunting feeling that he was doing wrong.

> Paul's advice is quite clear. *It is a Christian duty to think of everything, not as it affects ourselves only, but also as it affects others.* Now, note, that Paul is not saying that we must always allow our conduct to be dominated and dictated by the views, and even the prejudices, of others; there are matters which are essentially matters of principle, and in them a man must take his own way. But, there are a great many things which are neutral and indifferent; there are a great many things which are neither in themselves good or bad; there are a great many things which are really pleasures and pastimes, and habits and customs, which a man need not do unless he likes. They are not essential parts of life and conduct; they belong to what we might call the extras of life; and, it is Paul's conviction, that in such things we have no right to give offence to the more scrupulous brother. We have no right to distress and outrage his conscience by doing them ourselves, or by persuading him to do them.[3]

---

[3]*The Letter to the Romans* (*The Daily Study Bible*), translated and interpreted by William Barclay; Edinburgh: The Saint Andrew Press; Philadelphia: The Westminster Press; 1958; pp. 206, 207. Used by permission.

Meaning 15. How would you define a "stumbling block"?

Fact 16. Let's look more closely at this principle of not allowing our actions to harm another.

a) What ought we to strive for in our life? (vs. 17)

----

b) What ought we *not* to strive for? ----------------

----

c) Verse 19 adds what additional goal toward which we strive?

----

d) We do not want to do what according to verse 20?

We will never reach these four goals which Paul sets before us if we disregard the feelings of others. Barclay points this out very clearly.

There is *righteousness*, and righteousness consists in giving to men and to God what is their due. Now the very first thing that is due to a fellow man in the Christian life is sympathy and consideration. There is *peace*. In the New Testament peace does not mean simply absence of trouble; it means everything that makes for a man's highest good. If we insist that Christian freedom means doing what we like, we can never attain peace. There is *joy*. In Christianity joy can never be a selfish thing. Christian joy does not consist in making ourselves happy, it consists in making others happy.[4]

Fact   17. Verses 20-23 summarize Paul's argument. Read these as a summary.

Meaning 18. There are things which some Christians feel they cannot do, such as attending the movies, drinking moderately, smoking, dancing, or playing cards. Remembering the two principles:

a) How do you feel about each area? What does *your* conscience tell you?

_____

_____

_____

_____

b) If you feel free in these areas, when do you suppose you might harm another by acting upon your God-given freedom?

_____

_____

_____

[4]*Ibid.*, p. 209

c) Regardless of what you decide about these areas, remember the injunction not to judge or despise those who decide oppositely.

B. Significance

Let me summarize. The basis of our freedom as Christians is the fact that "nothing is unclean in itself" (vs. 14). Therefore it is permissible to do anything (except those things expressly forbidden such as murder and lying). However we do not do *all* things, because we are not "fully convinced" (vs. 5) that all things can be done to the "honour of the Lord" (vs. 6) nor that they result in "peace and mutual upbuilding" (vs. 19) or "joy in the Holy Spirit" (vs. 17). Likewise, we sometimes temper our actions because our liberty might harm our brother (vs. 15).

As Christians we are not bound by a long list of "do's" and "don'ts." We are *free to choose* how we act. In Paul's day, pagan man was bound. He had numerous regulations and restrictions which he followed in order to please his gods. Christ delivered man from all this and made him free. Rather than strict rules we have been given guidelines by which to order our lives. Let us apply these guidelines conscientiously.

Go back now to section A (Analysis) and add more principles to the list you have started.

FOR YOUR CONSIDERATION

What can a Christian do? Anything he pleases, as long as he loves God. Does this startle you? I hope it does. It is not original with me. St. Augustine said it first: "Love God, and then do as you please." Augustine did as he pleased *before* he loved God, so he was not speaking from a sheltered, fenced-in innocence, or naiveté. *But* Jesus Christ so captured his heart that *after* his conversion he could still do as he pleased. *If* we have exposed our hearts to the Heart that broke on Calvary for us, we are *drawn* into the "bright captivity" of love. In this "bright captivity" we find ourselves *free* to live. It does not happen overnight that a man or woman loves God enough so that he or she will only want to please Him. But it can and does happen. This I believe to be His highest will for us. His heart holds no rule book, but it does hold us, if we permit it.

You can go on doing those things, being that way, thinking those thoughts, but you do not even think *alone*. There is no private corner where you can go and think your own thoughts. God knows. This is a fact, not a theory. Whether you believe it, or like it, is beside the point. He is there. He knows.

But He is not there to cramp your style, to restrain you, to keep you *from*. He is there to free you, to loose you, so that you can always be going *toward* the abundant life. When Jesus spoke the words that raised His dear friend Lazarus from the dead, He made one telling comment: "Untie him, and give him a chance to move." This is totally characteristic of Jesus Christ. It still is. Always, in all ways, He is interested in your freedom to become all that you can become in Him.

External forms of conduct are not to be considered *first*. *You* are to be considered *first,* because *you* are first with God.

If you are allowing Him to love you into loving Him, as you *can* learn to love Him, you will find yourself moving toward the place where you will be able to love God and do as you please.

There is no delight on earth to compare with the free, open delight of the human heart when it is responding *naturally* to Jesus Christ.

The most creative and satisfying and joy-filled thing I know is to live so that we can look at Him, and be glad that He is looking back at us.

From *Find Out For Yourself*
by Eugenia Price
Grand Rapids: Zondervan Publishing House, pp. 150 & 151.

FOR YOUR BOOKSHELF

1. *Find Out for Yourself* by Eugenia Price; pp. 150 & 151.

2. *Consistent Christianity* by Michael C. Griffiths.
   A discussion of Christian behavior.

3. *The True Bounds of Christian Freedom* by Samuel Bolton; London: Banner of Truth Press.
   Samuel Bolton was a Puritan minister who lived around 1650. This is an interesting statement of the Puritan Doctrine of Christian Liberty.

4. *Taboo?* by C. S. Woods; Chicago: Inter-Varsity Press.
   A short booklet appraising common attitudes toward wordliness and discussing its biblical meaning.